piano • vocal • guitar

jennifer knapp

ISBN 0-634-04435-4

HAL•LEONARD®
CORPORATION

7777 W. BLUEMOUND RD. P.O. BOX 13819 MILWAUKEE, WI 53213

Visit Hal Leonard Online at
www.halleonard.com

BY AND BY

Words and Music by
JENNIFER KNAPP

Original key: E minor. This edition has been transposed up one half-step to be more playable.

BREATHE ON ME

Words and Music by
JENNIFER KNAPP

Guitar: Drop D tuning:
(low to high) D-A-D-G-B-E

Slowly, with a beat

No temp - ta - tion seize a man _ that he _ _ can't o - ver - come. _ Who am I _ _ to be fall - en?

Crack Your back _ on a slab of wood; _ come free - dom, nail it down. _ I come crawl -

THE WAY I AM

Words and Music by
JENNIFER KNAPP

SAY WON'T YOU SAY

Words and Music by
JENNIFER KNAPP

AROUND ME

Words and Music by
JENNIFER KNAPP

If all the worlds were scat-tered and __ I found my way to here, then
One big bang, an at-om I? __ Oh, how'd I come to be? then

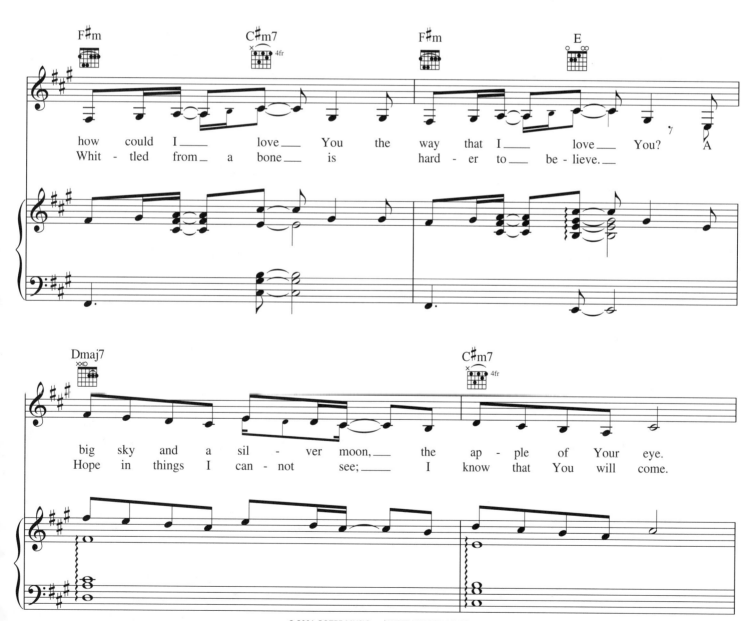

how could I __ love __ You the way that I __ love __ You?
Whit-tled from __ a bone __ is hard-er to __ be-lieve. __

big sky and a sil-ver moon, __ the ap-ple of Your eye.
Hope in things I can-not see; __ I know that You will come.

COME TO ME

Words and Music by
JENNIFER KNAPP

Leaves a mind left to won - der where the world's she gone.
The great be - yond, a bet - ter mys - t'ry than the life at hand.

Once her head laced in ha - los; how could it go wrong?
Search the shad - ows, on - ly to find a dry and wea - ry land.

CHARITY

Words and Music by
JENNIFER KNAPP

Love __ me;
Whis - per;

for - get me not.
say my name.

Hold __ me up, ___
All ___ I've dreamed __

Ho - ly Rock.
re - main un - changed.

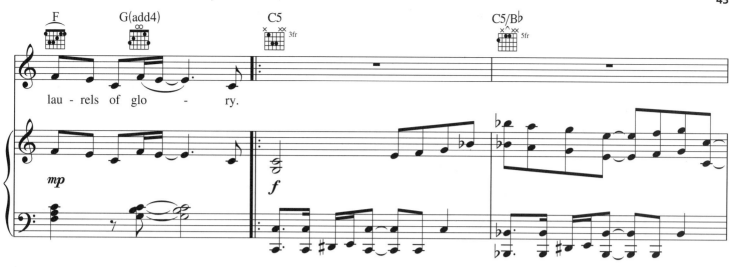

lau - rels of glo - ry.

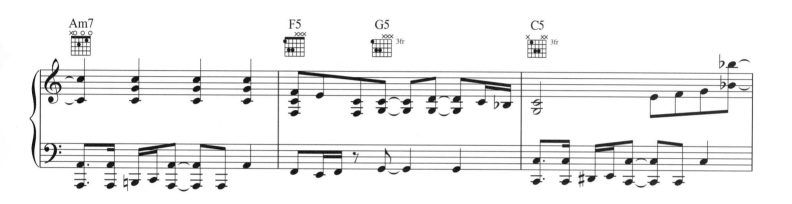

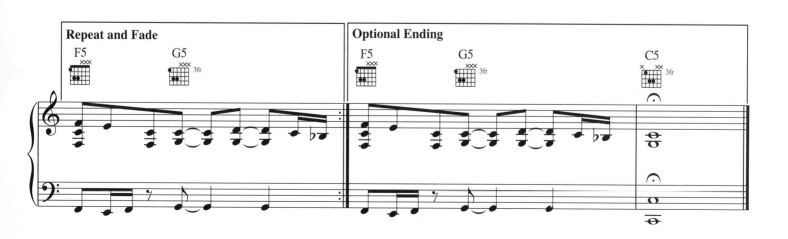

FALL DOWN

Words and Music by
JENNIFER KNAPP

SING MARY SING

Words and Music by
JENNIFER KNAPP

Guitar: Drop D tuning, Capo II
(low to high) D-A-D-G-B-E

Slow Pop

Mar - y had a ba - by___ born in a man - ger.
Her - od with a vi - sion,___ out with a ven - geance.

Mar - y, what to do? Mar - y,___ what___ to do?___ Be -
Mar - y, what to do? Mar - y,___ what___ to do?___ Oh,

IN TWO
(The Lament)

Words and Music by
JENNIFER KNAPP

LIGHT OF THE WORLD

Words and Music by
JENNIFER KNAPP

Additional Lyrics

Answer me...
Answer me...
Answer me when I call to You, oh my righteous God.
Give me relief from all distress.
Be merciful to me, and hear my prayer.
How long, oh men, will you turn my glory into shame, my glory into shame?
How long will you love delusions and seek false gods?
Know that the Lord has set apart the godly for Himself.
When I call to Him...
In your anger, do not sin.
When you are on your bed, search your heart and be silent.
Offer right sacrifices and trust in the Lord
When you're asking who can show us in Your Word.
You have filled my heart with greater joy
Than when their grain and new wine abound.
I will lie down and sleep in peace,
For You alone, You alone, oh Lord
Make me dwell in safety, dwell in safety.

"I am the Light of the world.
Whoever follows me will never walk in darkness,
But will have the light of life."

NO REGRETS

Words and Music by
JENNIFER KNAPP